TOOLS FOR TEACHERS

- **ATOS:** 0.5
- **GRL:** A
- **LEXILE:** BR10L

- **CURRICULUM CONNECTIONS:** animals
- **WORD COUNT:** 44

Skills to Teach

- **HIGH-FREQUENCY WORDS:** a, is, jumps, plays, runs
- **CONTENT WORDS:** born, cries, drinks, grazes, grows, lamb, nurses, shivers, sleeps, snuggles, stands, wakes
- **PUNCTUATION:** periods
- **WORD STUDY:** silent *b* (*lamb*); *r*-controlled vowels (*nurses*, *shivers*); /ng/, spelled *in* (*drinks*)
- **TEXT TYPE:** factual recount

Before Reading Activities

- Read the title and give a simple statement of the main idea.
- Have students "walk" though the book and talk about what they see in the pictures.
- Introduce new vocabulary by having students predict the first letter and locate the word in the text.
- Discuss any unfamiliar concepts that are in the text.

After Reading Activities

Encourage children to talk about the different things lambs are shown doing in the book. List the different behaviors, such as grazing, nursing, sleeping, and jumping, on the board and consider which farm babies (piglets, foals, calves, etc.) might do the same things. Would a calf nurse? How about a chick? Following the children's suggestions, write the animal's name underneath the behavior.

Tadpole Books are published by Jump!, 5357 Penn Avenue South, Minneapolis, MN 55419, www.jumplibrary.com

Copyright ©2018 Jump. International copyright reserved in all countries. No part of this book may be reproduced in any form without written permission from the publisher.

Editor: Jenny Fretland VanVoorst **Designer:** Anna Peterson

Photo Credits: Alamy: FL collection, 10; Dreamstime: Tommy Beattie, 6–7. Getty: Peter Cade, 4; Joao Inacio, 5; Menno Boermans, 8. Shutterstock: Djem, cover; Eric Isselee, 1; Elliot Photography 2, 3; Darren Baker, 9; Bluskystudio, 11; Holly Kuchera, 12–13; photobars, 14; 1000 Words, 15.

Library of Congress Cataloging-in-Publication Data
Names: Mayerling, Tim, author.
Title: Lambs / by Tim Mayerling.
Description: Minneapolis, MN: Jump!, Inc., (2017) | Series: Farm babies | Audience: Ages 3–6. | Includes index.
Identifiers: LCCN 2017019980 (print) | LCCN 2017001200 (ebook) | ISBN 9781624966163 (ebook) | ISBN 9781620317693 (hardcover: alk. paper) | ISBN 9781620317891 (pbk.)
Subjects: LCSH: Lambs—Juvenile literature.
Classification: LCC SF376.5 (print) | LCC SF376.5 .M39 2017 (ebook) | DDC 636.3/07—dc23
LC record available at https://lccn.loc.gov/2017019980

LAMBS

by Tim Mayerling

TABLE OF CONTENTS

tadpole
books

LAMBS

lamb

A lamb is born.

A lamb stands.

A lamb cries.

A lamb nurses.

A lamb sleeps.

A lamb wakes.

A lamb shivers.

A lamb snuggles.

A lamb drinks.

A lamb grazes.

A lamb runs.

A lamb jumps.

A lamb plays.

A lamb grows.

WORDS TO KNOW

cry

graze

jump

nurse

run

sleep

INDEX